Hastings To

By
Nick Hanna and Tim Cross

Photography by
Andrew Catlin, John Cole, Tim Cross, Käthe Deutsch, Steven Differ, George Greaves, Peter Greenhalf and Janet Pollard, Nick Hanna, Roland Jarvis, Peter Johns, John Kenward, Bob Mazzer, John Miles, Denise O'Neil, Chris Parker, Steve Pyke, Camilla Stapleton-Hibbert, Nick Wates and Anna White

Map by Martin Honeysett

seachange
PUBLISHING

Hastings Today

This first edition published December 2001 by
Seachange Publishing, 13 Old Humphrey Avenue, Hastings, East Sussex TN34 3BT

© Nick Hanna and Tim Cross 2001. 120pp
© in photographs remains with individual photographers

All rights reserved. No reproduction permitted without the prior permission of the publisher

ISBN: 0-9541872-0-2

Printed in England by Miro Press
Printed on paper from sustainable forests

This book would not have been possible without the generous co-operation of all the photographers involved, and we are very grateful for their patience and the goodwill which they have shown towards the project throughout. We would particularly like to thank Nick Wates for his creative input to the overall concept and his considerable contribution to the development process. Thanks also to Jeremy Brook for his invaluable contribution. For their support, encouragement and advice we would also like to thank Kevin Boorman, Lesley Cornish, Stephanie Donaldson, Simon Gooch, Nick Marshall, Penny Precious, and Lorraine Roberts. To the best of our knowledge the information in this book is accurate. The publishers can accept no responsibility for any errors and omissions.

Introduction	6
Map	8
Combe Haven	10
West St Leonards	12
St George's Day	14
St Leonards	16
Burton's St Leonards	20
Hastings Museum	24
Pier and White Rock	26
May Day	32
The America Ground	38
Town Centre	40
Sports	44
Alexandra Park	48
Castle and West Hill	53
St Clement's Caves	54
Music	56
Pelham Boulevard	58
The Beach	60
Lifeboat	64
Shorething Festival	66
George Street	68
Old Town	70
Seagulls	78
Hastings Week	80
The Stade	88
Coastal Currents	96
Fishermen	98
Hastings Week	104
Urban Woodland	106
Bonfire	108
Country Park	114
Christmas	118

Introduction

This book is a celebration of Hastings and St Leonards, one of Britain's best-known seaside resorts, and the many fascinating aspects of its heritage, townscapes, cultural life, and colourful annual events.

Hastings is closely associated with one of the most famous events in English history, the Battle of Hastings, which witnessed the birth of the nation as William of Normandy defeated Harold to gain the English throne in 1066.

Under the Normans, Hastings prospered as one of the prestigious Cinque Ports, but it suffered a setback when severe storms silted up the harbour in the 13th century, and it was further ravaged by the French during the Hundred Years War.

There was a revival in the 16th century when Hastings supplied ships for the Armada. Thanks to its proximity to the French coast, the town was a hotbed of smuggling during the 18th and early 19th centuries.

Hastings' role as a seaside resort began at the beginning of the 19th century as the Victorians discovered the benefits of clean, seaside air. The building of most of modern Hastings and St Leonards as we know it today dates from this era.

Although Hastings was heavily bombed during the war, it has still retained a remarkable architectural legacy not only from Victorian times but also dating back several centuries - the oldest building in the old town was built in 1450.

No other seaside town in Britain can rival this rich heritage, or the historical background to its fishing fleet, which has been in existence for more than a millennium.

But Hastings is not just about history - on the contrary, it has a thriving contemporary artistic and cultural scene which finds expression in a wealth of exhibitions, events and live performances. Indeed, it is now becoming almost as famous for its creative flair in staging festivals as it has been for giving its name to the battle. As well as the events portrayed in this book it also plays host to a Dance Festival (February), an International Poetry Festival (November), and the International Chess Congress (December and January).

Hastings is fortunate in its wonderful natural environment, which includes not only five kilometres of unspoiled beach but also the delights of Alexandra Park in the middle of the town and of Combe Haven and the Country Park on its outskirts. Its wooded valleys even provide the town with its own micro-climate.

In recent years Hastings has had more than its fair share of negative publicity, largely focusing on social problems. Now, however, over £36 million is being invested in regeneration, improvements and social action. The town is being rediscovered as one of the south coast's best kept secrets.

There is much to celebrate and enjoy about this raffish, good-natured, idiosyncratic, cosmopolitan and entertaining place - and this book is your invitation to do so.

Nick Hanna and Tim Cross
Hastings Old Town, December 2001

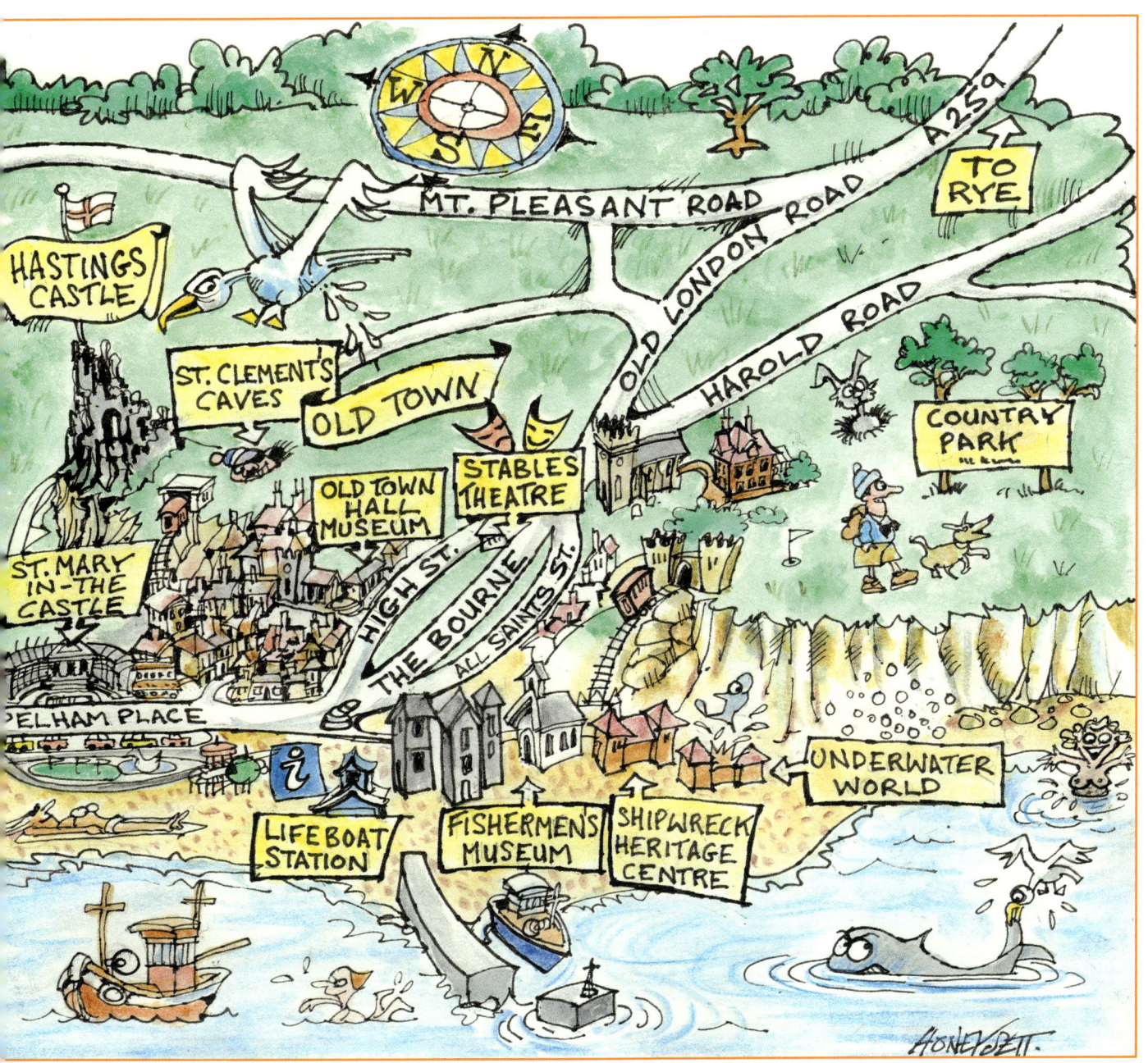

Combe Haven Valley

The Combe Haven Valley, on the very western edge of the borough, is a hidden gem. A refuge for wildlife, this nature reserve is of national importance and is designated as a Site of Special Scientific Interest (SSSI). The proposed Hastings by-pass would have run through its heart.

The valley is predominantly farmland which floods extensively in winter, creating lowland marsh habitats. It includes an extensive network of drainage canals and reedbeds, the Filsham Reedbed, which is one of the country's top wetland reserves, home to a wide variety of flora and fauna. The drier slopes of the valley feature grassland meadows and ancient woodlands.

Over 100 species of birds frequent Combe Haven, with at least 35 species (including the bearded tit, water rail and reed and sedge warblers) breeding on the marshes. Water rails and bearded tits in particular are thriving here, and it's hoped that spotted crakes and marsh warblers will also soon be breeding. Predators hunting through the reedbeds include marsh and hen harriers, as well as long-eared and short-eared owls.

During the summer, the valley is alive with brightly-coloured dragonflies, which can be seen flitting around the banks of the Combe Haven in their eye-catching, iridescent colours. Over 20 of Britain's dragonfly species have been recorded here, making it one of the most important sites in the country for these insects.

The Filsham Reedbed is currently undergoing a five year restoration project, managed by the Sussex Wildlife Trust, which aims to reinstate it as a breeding site for bitterns. Known for their booming call, there are only 22 breeding pairs left in Britain of this famously secretive brown heron. The £138,000 scheme will also include new paths (with disabled access), footbridges, and other facilities.

West St Leonards

Bulverhythe beach is home to a small fleet of fishing boats and rows of traditional seaside bathing huts. The shingle beach and maritime cliffs, home to rare plants such as sea kale and long-horned poppy, is one of several of the town's nature reserves to benefit from recent grants to improve habitats and create on-site art projects under the Greenspace Project.

One of the most famous shipwrecks on the Sussex coastline lies in the sands of Bulverhythe. The *Amsterdam* is a Dutch East Indiaman which beached here on January 26, 1749. She had set sail from her home port in the Netherlands just two weeks previously, bound for Java with a cargo of wine, silver and cloth. No sooner had she entered the English Channel than she was struck by a violent gale and driven into Pevensey Bay, where she lost her rudder and ran aground. Her 250-year old timbers can be seen at very low tides. Artefacts recovered from the wreck are on display in the Shipwreck Heritage Centre (p93).

West Marina marks the beginning of the mile-long promenade linking St Leonards with the town centre, as well as the start of the popular seafront cycleway which forms part of National Route 2 on the cycle network. In Grosvenor Gardens, alongside the bowling green, there's a statue of the dying King Harold being cradled by his wife, Enid.

St George's Day

A recent addition to the town's calendar of events is a colourful celebration of St George's Day, which falls in late April. St George is the patron saint of England who, according to legend, rescued a princess by slaying a fearsome dragon. The tale of the maiden's rescue is re-enacted with gusto in Warrior Square, with performances and costumes courtesy of the Hastings Borough Bonfire Society and the Creative Arts Centre. This celebration of all things English also includes a ceremonial procession, a medieval fayre, medieval games in the square, Morris dancing and a display of the chivalric arts.

St Leonards-on-Sea has been part of the borough of Hastings since 1885, although many residents feel that it has its own distinctive, Bohemian character (not least because one of its central thoroughfares is called Bohemia Road).

One of the first planned seaside towns, St Leonards was developed by the distinguished London architect James Burton, who began building here in 1828. The Royal Victoria Hotel (right) was one of his original showpiece buildings (formerly known as the St Leonards Hotel, it was re-named following a visit by Queen Victoria). A stroll around St Leonards will reveal many more examples of Burton's work.

Marine Court (left) is a landmark building on the south coast. Completed in 1937 at the height of the Art Deco movement, it was one of the first residential buildings in the country to be constructed using a steel frame and concrete. Marine Court was commissioned just one year after the launch of the *Queen Mary* and many believe it's unusual design was influenced by that prestigious liner. The 12-storey block (which accommodates 160 flats, 20 shops, and offices) was given listed building status in 1999. Marina Pavilion, set beneath the promenade opposite Marine Court, is a popular venue for local bands.

The gardens in Warrior Square (overleaf, bottom left), which have recently been renovated, are renowned for their roses.

St Leonards

Burton's St Leonards

St Leonards has a rich architectural heritage which reflects the glamour and ambition of the Victorian gentry who created this seaside resort - in particular, it bears the signature of the celebrated London architect, James Burton.

St Leonards is unusual in that it was the first new town in the country to have landscaped open spaces incorporated in the planning. Burton's vision encompassed an eclectic range of styles (including Greek classical, Scottish baronial and various Gothic influences) and many of these well-preserved buildings can still be seen on a stroll around the town. Amongst the more prominent are the Royal Victoria Hotel, the Masonic Hall, Crown House, the Clock House, North Lodge, and Gloucester Lodge. Burton's work was carried on after his death by his equally talented son, Decimus Burton. The Burton family tomb is a distinctive pyramid which sits on the hill behind the parish church.

Cottages at Mount Pleasant (left) were originally lived in by construction workers building Burton's new town. Nearby Mercatoria was the mercantile or tradesmen's area, whilst Lavatoria (now part of Norman Road) was the laundry district.

Burton's St Leonards

Hastings Musuem

Hastings Museum and Art Gallery contains a variety of displays relating to local history, wildlife, artists and writers, as well as the cultures of other lands. The most spectacular part of the museum is the magnificent Durbar Hall, originally built for the Indian and Colonial Exhibition in 1886.

The museum possesses an early 'televisor' and scanning disk used by John Logie Baird, the inventor of television, who is said to have been inspired whilst walking in the Country Park. In 1923 he made a breakthrough in transmitting moving images at his Hastings home - an experiment which led to the development of the most important communications medium of the 20th century. A set of rare, historic letters written by Baird was acquired by the museum in 1999.

Displays on Native American culture reflect the fact that Hastings was the birthplace of one of the earliest environmental campaigners, the Canadian conservationist known as Grey Owl (1888-1938). The 'Hastings Indian', whose real name was Archie Belaney, was immortalised in the film *Grey Owl* (2000).

Pier and White Rock

Hastings pier re-opened in 2001 after extensive refurbishment and is now once again a focal point of the seafront promenade with thriving shops, bars and cafés. Designed by one of the great Victorian pier engineers, Eugenius Birch, the 900ft long pier first opened on August 5, 1872 (Britain's first ever Bank Holiday). Its ballroom played host to some of the great names in vaudeville (including Marie Lloyd and George Robey) and during the 1960s and '70s famous acts such as The Rolling Stones, Jimi Hendrix, The Kinks, The Who and Pink Floyd played here.

Over the years the pier has undergone many changes. It was nearly destroyed by fire in 1917. It closed in October 1999 when the previous owners went bankrupt and subsequent storm damage meant that over 500 tons of structural steel had to be replaced before its new owners could re-open to the public. Today, it not only provides the traditional pleasures of a stroll above the waves but also plays host to artistic and cultural events.

Between the pier and the America Ground is an area known as White Rock, after a massive sandstone headland which once stood here (it was demolished in 1835 to make way for the promenade). Behind the pier is the White Rock Theatre and White Rock Gardens, which includes the Clambers play centre and Falaise Fitness Centre.

Beneath the prom, running from the pier to Warrior Square, Bottle Alley was built in 1933 and, as the name implies, it's decorated with thousands of pieces of coloured glass.

Pier and White Rock

Pier and White Rock

May Day

The May Day Bank Holiday marks the beginning of the summer tourist season with the exuberant Jack in the Green celebrations. The town also fills up with thousands of bikers, leading to the curious spectacle of leather-clad motorcylists and costumed Morris dancers mingling en masse in the town's pubs. The annual bike run to Hastings started around 1990 and now attracts anything between 10-15,000 bikers. It's a thrilling sight as gleaming machines of every description seem to gradually fill up every spare inch of space along the seafront.

Jack in the Green is an ancient tradition to mark the end of winter which was revived in the early 1980s in Hastings. It has since grown into the largest event of its kind anywhere in the world, featuring four days of entertainment, music, ribald revellery, dancing and merry-making in the streets. This extraordinary and sometimes bewildering event attracts around 1,500 Morris dancers and other participants, with over 10,000 spectators watching the final procession.

The main celebrations revolve around The Jack, a massive 'dancing bush' bedecked with flowers and ribbons, which has to be slain in order to release the spirit of summer. Jack is accompanied on his journey by his loud, belligerent friends the Bogeys (who clear the way for him with their noisy drumming) and his consort, Black Sal. Also in the procession is the Fat Man with a Drum (who wears red), and the Sweeps, because the end of winter also meant a new season of chimney cleaning.

May Day

34

An important part of the Jack in the Green procession are the fabulous dancing Giants, their towering size adding an even more dramatic touch to the event. Jack is released from the Fishermen's Museum and the procession makes its way around the town - with numerous stops for ritual beer drinking - before he is slaughtered in the Castle. The origins of today's May Day celebrations lie deep in Anglo-Saxon history and the noise, dancing, and passion of the event give it a highly charged, primal atmosphere.

Kawasaki
YAMAHA
KAWASAKI
SUZUKI

Q168 KCP
M982 XUM
W799 BKM
POLICE

The America Ground

The America Ground is an unusual corner of the town centre which has its own particular history. In the early 19th century Hastings was unndergoing rapid expansion but the labourers brought in to work on the building of Pelham Crescent, Wellington Square and other projects had nowhere to live, so many of them squatted on vacant land here. Within a decade this had become a shanty town of over 1,000 people, many living in lean-to's, old boat hulks, and other ramshackle buildings. The area gained a reputation for drunkenness and lawlessness but when the authorities stepped in to restore order they met with considerable hostility. Residents hoisted the Stars and Stripes as a symbol of their independence and, since then, it's been known as the America Ground.

After an inquiry which concluded that the land belonged to the Crown (to this day property owners still pay rent to the Queen), the squatters were cleared and building work began. The Holy Trinity Church was completed in 1858 and the Brassey Institute (which now houses the library) in 1878.

The America Ground recently underwent a £620,000 facelift, with the installation of period-style street lights and paving stones. A new mural has also been completed. The area hosts lively street markets (including the occasional French market, and a Christmas market).

In July America's Independence Day is celebrated with live bands, re-enactments of the area's history, children's activities, fashion shows, and street entertainments.

39

Town Centre

Most of Hastings' town centre is a pedestrianised zone, so you can stroll on traffic-free roads between its shops, cafés, pubs, and restaurants.

The main shopping centre, Priory Meadow (right), opened in 1997. It was built on the site of a famous cricket ground, which is commemorated by the statue of a cricketer in its precinct.

Alongside Priory Meadow is the Town Hall, which houses the main Information Centre. On one corner of the Town Hall there's a small stone kiosk selling snacks: curiously, this was one of the original ticket kiosks when part of Priory Meadow was a coach station in the 1950s.

Opposite the Town Hall, Queen's Avenue (left) is an elegant forerunner of the main shopping centre. It was the site of John Logie Baird's workshop (Baird's main residence was at 23, Linton Crescent).

JOHN LOGIE BAIRD
1888 – 1946
DISPLAYED THE FIRST TELEVISION IMAGES IN THIS HOUSE IN 1923
THE INSTITUTE OF PHYSICS

Town centre

Wellington Square (above) is a prime example of elegant Georgian architecture and dates from the early 1800s when Hastings first became popular as a fashionable seaside resort.

The town centre is as busy at night as it is by day, with plenty of convivial pubs and wine bars including French's, Walker's, Yates' Wine Lodge, the Street, Harper's, Trader Jack's, Pissaro's and the John Logie Baird. If you want a bit of history with your drink drop in to the Havelock, which is famous for its rare tile panels. The four, hand-painted tile murals date from the turn of the century and are Grade II listed (top right).

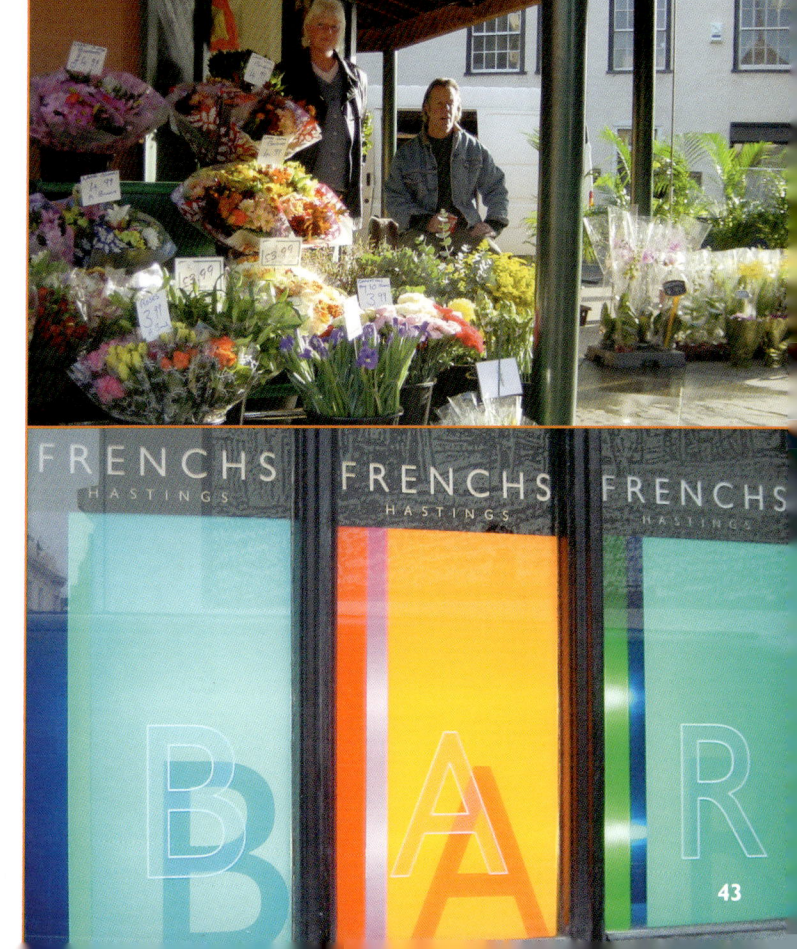

Sports

Hastings has a wide range of sporting facilities and an active sporting community. Sports centres include the Summerfields Leisure Centre, the Falaise Fitness Centre, Hillcrest Sports Centre, and the YMCA Sports Centre. Tennis lawns and courts are situated in Alexandra Park and White Rock Gardens. There are several putting greens as well as the Hastings Golf and Country Club (located in Beauport Park on the northern outskirts of town).

The Hastings half-marathon attracts top class participants and is often referred to as the Great South Run.

Bowling is very popular and there are well-kept greens in Alexandra Park, White Rock Gardens, and Grosvenor Gardens. During 2002 a new £1.3 million indoor bowls centre is being built at White Rock Gardens.

The jewel in the crown of the town's sports facilities is the new Horntye Park sports complex (left and top right) on Bohemia Road. It features a county standard cricket arena, floodlit all-weather pitch, sports hall, and function facilities.

The White Rock Gardens skate park (overleaf), which features seven ramps and a ply surface, is hugely popular with local youngsters. Built by one of Europe's leading ramp designers after extensive consultations with the town's young people, the £20,000 park is suitable for BMXs, skateboards and rollerblades. Amongst the highly skilled users of the park are some of the country's leading underground and professional BMXers.

Sports

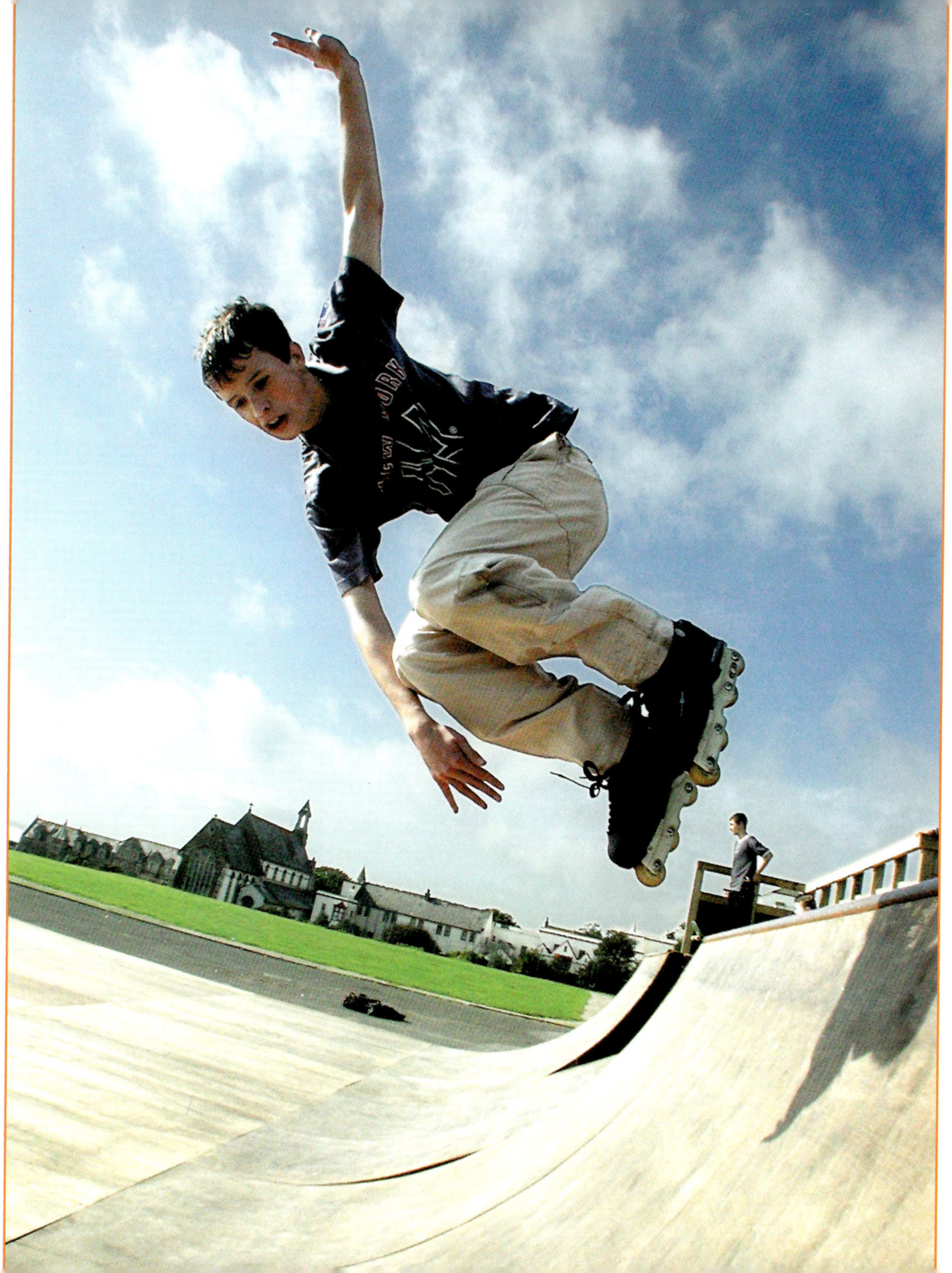

Alexandra Park

Snaking its way for three kilometres down a river valley in the centre of Hastings, Alexandra Park is the town's most important public park. Designed by the pre-eminent landscape designer, Robert Marnock, it was officially opened by Princess Alexandra in June 1882. The park contains more than 300 rare and exotic trees, thirty of which are classified as 'champion species' - these are mostly oaks, cedars and redwoods which are amongst the largest of their kind in the country.

The 50 hectare (120 acre) park is unusual because of the way it gradually changes from formal gardens in the south to wilderness areas in the north. The latter include Coronation Wood and Old Roar Ghyll (a small ravine with ancient woodland and rare plant species), both of which are nature reserves which were joined to the park in 1996.

This green oasis, one of the most spectacular Victorian parks of its day, is currently undergoing a three-year regeneration programme to restore its former splendour. The project involves renewing the Victorian railings, restoring the bandstand, dredging and rejuvenating the three ponds, refurbishing the park café, providing new visitor facilities, and restoring many historic features as well as watercourses, reservoirs, natural habitats, and shrubberies. The £3.4m project is due for completion in 2003.

This much-loved park hosts the long-established Hastings Beer Festival (July), outdoor band concerts (every Sunday in July and August) and children's activities such as the annual 'Let's Go to the Park' fun day and summer's 'Playdays in the Park'.

Alexandra Park

50

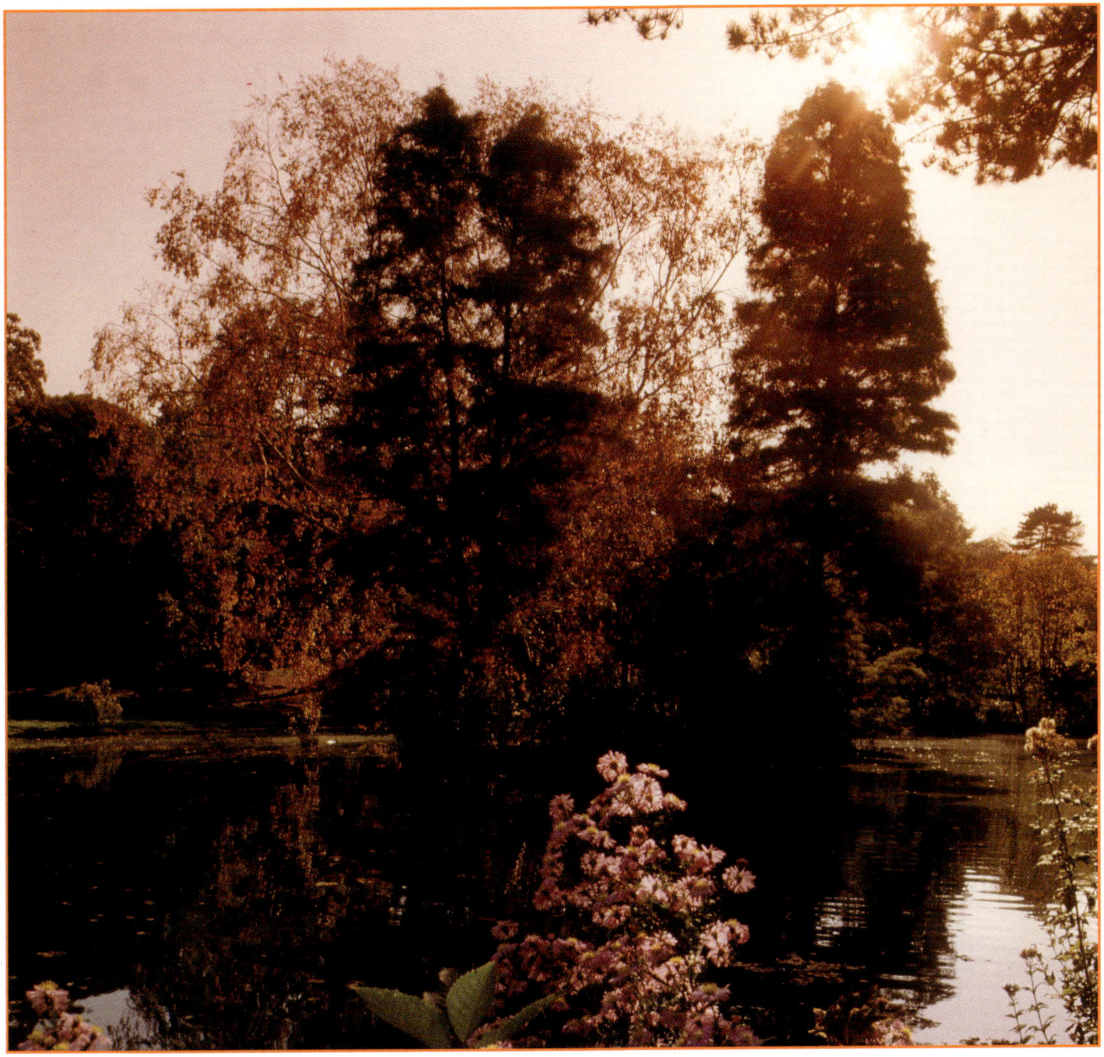

Castle and West Hill

52

The ruins of Hastings castle stand high atop the West Hill, a fragmented reminder of the town's strategic importance in centuries past. The castle, which was the first to be built after the Norman Conquest, was once a mighty structure covering nearly five hectares (11 acres). It was completed in 1067.

In 1070 Robert, Count of Eu, built a collegiate church inside the castle walls. The remains of this church form the best preserved part of the castle today.

The castle was partially dismantled by King John in 1216, then rebuilt by Henry III in 1225. In the late 13th century violent storms changed the coastline to the extent that Hastings lost its harbour; from then onwards the castle had little military significance and fell into decay. The church, however, remained in use until the reign of Henry VIII. A large proportion of the castle was lost when the cliff was cut back in the 19th century.

From inside the castle there are wonderful views over the town and coast. An audio-visual presentation, the 1066 Experience, relates the castle's history. Near the entrance there are two dungeons hewn out of the sandstone, the so-called 'whispering dungeons'.

To the east of the castle is an area of open ground known as the Ladies Parlour, so called because when jousting tournaments were held here they would be staged under the auspices of a lady of nobility.

St Clement's Caves

Covering more than 5,000 square metres under the West Hill, St Clement's Caves consist of an upper cavern and an extensive interlocking area of lower caverns. Most of the caves were excavated for sandstone (used for glass-making), and they were almost certainly used by smugglers in the 18th century. In 1797 they were enlarged to create a military hospital but then blocked up and forgotten about until Joseph Golding, a local greengrocer, re-discovered them by accident in 1825.

Thus begun a lifelong obsession, as Golding carved out yet more caverns as well as the incredible Monk's Walk (this page), a 44 metre-long passage with 23 niches, each flanked by pillars. Supernatural apparitions occur in the caves on a regular basis.

During World War II the caves were used as an air-raid shelter and school; in the post-War years they were a popular venue for jazz concerts and tea dances. In 1989 they were converted into the Smugglers Adventure, an interactive exhibition about smuggling on the south coast.

Music

Nana Tsiboe

Lynda Murray

Lainee Carroll

The town has a thriving live music scene, embracing everything from jazz to rock, folk, classical and world music. Local musicians and bands play regularly in pubs and clubs such as the Crypt, Fubar, French's, the Yelton, the Carlisle, Pissaro's, Smuggler's, and Harper's in the town centre, as well as at larger venues such as St-Mary-in-the-Castle, the Phoenix Arts Centre and the Marina Pavilion.

In the old town there are regular blues, folk, jazz, rock and bluegrass nights in pubs and bars which include the Stag, the Hastings Arms, Porter's, the London Trader, the Crown, the Jenny Lind, the Anchor, and the First In Last Out.

Liam Genockey

Steve Riv

Trevor Watts and Marcus Cummins

John Ballard

The White Rock Theatre is the venue for the Hastings Music Festival (March), a competition for both adults and children. The Black Horse Music Festival (May) is a popular event featuring rock, blues and folk, held just outside town in Telham. St-Mary-in-the-Castle hosts the Hastings International Blues Festival (September), which was inaugurated in 1999.

Pelham Boulevard

58

Connecting the pedestrian areas of the town centre with George Street and the old town, this section of the seafront is set to become a continental-style boulevard.

Pelham Crescent, built in 1824 by Jospeh Kaye for the Earl of Chichester, is a fine example of Georgian architecture. Sadly, parts of the castle were lost when the rock face was cut away to make room for it.

The centrepiece of Pelham Crescent is St Mary-in-the-Castle, a beautiful late Georgian church built into the cliff which is lit by a glass dome in the rotunda (left). This recently restored building is now one of Hastings' premier arts and entertainment venues, hosting professional orchestras as well as touring ensembles for jazz, blues, classical and world music and the popular jazz breakfasts and coffee concerts on Sunday mornings. The crypt is often used for art exhibitions.

Facing St Mary's and Pelham Crescent, a new decorative lighting scheme (above right) adds a stylish note to the seafront. The columns' wave-like reflectors are lit from beneath through coloured filters which change with the sea breezes.

The Beach

Hastings has benefited enormously from the recent completion of a £100 million scheme by Southern Water to improve waste water treatment in the town, and the seas are now cleaner than they have been for years. Indeed, a family of bottlenose dolphins has been seen regularly in recent summers as they come in to feed off shoals of mackerel in the inshore waters (the best places for spotting them are from the pier or Rock-a-Nore beach).

From May to September the town's 15 lifeguards are on constant patrol along the beach and foreshore between Rock-a-Nore and West Marina, and from July onwards there is a staffed lifeguard station at Pelham Place. The station provides a focal point for beach activities and as well as monitoring sea conditions and providing first aid the lifeguards are on hand to dispense directions and advice. They also hand out free sunblock lotion, thanks to the generosity of a local manufacturer. Hastings is the first seaside resort in Britain to provide this service. Weather permitting, the lifeguard boat patrols the shore on a daily basis.

Improvements in water quality and the introduction of the lifeguard station and other facilities meant that Hastings gained the prestigious European Seaside Award for the first time in 2001.

Tourism is one of the most important industries in Hastings and St Leonards, directly supporting around 3,000 jobs and bringing £100 million into the local economy annually.

The resort welcomes around two million day trippers and 300,000 staying visitors every year. Overseas language students are a very important part of the hospitality market, with around 45,000 students coming here every year to improve their English in the town's 45 language schools. The students, who come from all over the world, add a cosmopolitan atmosphere to Hastings during the summer.

The Beach

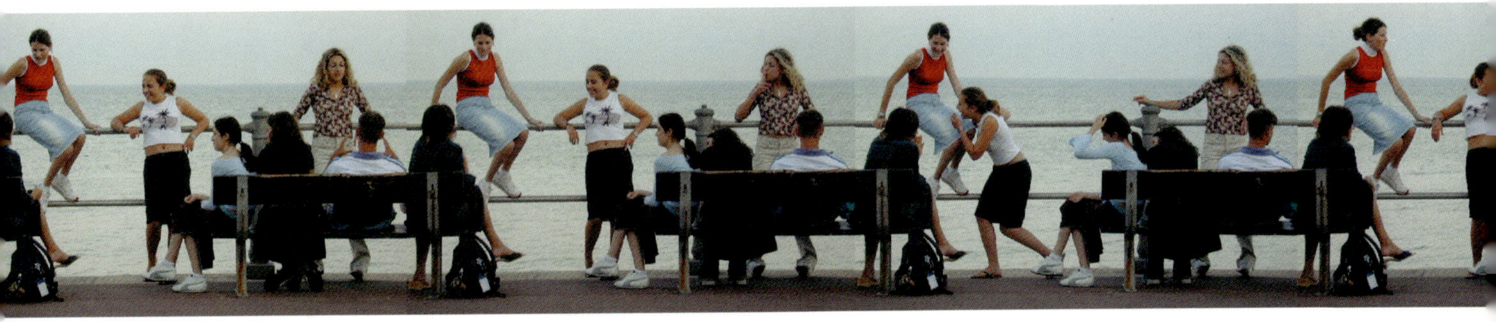

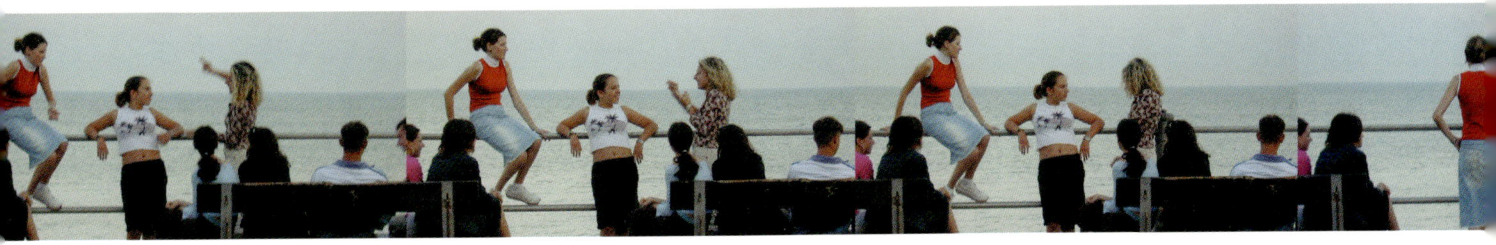

Lifeboat

Since it opened in 1996, Hastings' lifeboat station has become one of the most heavily-visited in the country, with around 10,000 annual visitors. It was specially designed to showcase the work of the Royal National Lifeboat Institution (RNLI) and has full disabled access.

The station was first established in 1858; since then its lifeboats have launched over 1400 times and saved nearly 500 lives. Currently it's two boats are the 12m, all-weather *Sealink Endeavour* and the 5m inshore lifeboat *Cecile Rampton II*. The station is staffed by 19 sea-going and 12 land-based volunteers.

Shorething Festival

The most recent addition to Hastings' growing roster of colourful, innovative events is the Shorething Festival of the sea, which takes place in July. Inaugurated in 2001, this creative celebration of life by the seaside includes events as diverse as beach art and sandcastle competitions, beach volleyball, sailing, canoeing and swimming races, and lifeguard demonstrations. Fish cookery shows and a continental market provide a backdrop to dancing, drumming, and choral performances.

The festival features a Birdman competition and a Tubman competition (the latter is in memory of a famous local character, Biddy the Tubman, who used to entertain day-trippers with his antics in a floating tub). Shorething also encompasses the well-established Walking the Fish parade, a colourful carnival (with lively Samba music) of over 600 costumed schoolchildren carrying giant fantastical sea creatures designed in collaboration with the arts group, Radiator.

George Street

George Street was originally a suburb of the old town - indeed, when it was first built outside of the town walls in the 17th century it was called the Suburbs. This busy pedestrianised street is now home to numerous pubs, cafés and restaurants and a wide variety of shops.

At the western end of George Street a passageway leads through to the Hundred Steps, which ascend to the West Hill. An alternative route is to take the West Hill cliff railway, which travels up through a 110 metre brick-lined tunnel and a natural cave before it emerges alongside the Ladies Parlour.

Old Town

Nestling in the Bourne valley and sheltered by the East and West Hills, Hastings old town has remained virtually unchanged in its outline for centuries. Originally it had just two main streets, High Street and All Saint's Street, separated by the Bourne stream. The stream was covered over in the 19th century and the old town was divided in two when the present-day main road was built along the course of the stream in the 1960s.

Because of its position between the two hills the old town developed as a tightly-knit network of lanes and alleyways as early builders sought to make use of every available space. These stepped or sloping passageways (known as 'twittens') give the old town a distinctive character as a stroll through its streets reveals half-hidden gardens, courtyards and old houses.

Old Town

There are many fine buildings in the old town, ranging from timber-framed medieval houses to the Victorian, and three churches. The oldest of these is the borough church of St Clement's (far left), built in 1380, which is dedicated to the patron saint of mariners. All Saint's Church (near left) was built around 1400, whilst the Roman Catholic Church of St Mary Star of the Sea was completed in 1883.

Famous residents of the old town have included the Duke of Wellington (1769-1852); poet Coventry Patmore (1823-1896); poet and artist Dante Gabriel Rossetti (1828-1882); Victorian traveller and artist Marianne North (1830-1890); self-proclaimed satanist Aleister Crowley (1875-1947); painter John Bratby (1928-1992); and the novelist Catherine Cookson (1906-1998). The old town was also home to two pioneering female doctors: Elizabeth Blackwell (1821-1910), one of the first female professors of gynaecology, and Sophie Jex Blake (1840-1912), who founded the Royal Free Hospital.

Old Town

At the heart of the old town is the High Street, which was the commercial centre of Hastings until the modern town was built. Today it is a thriving hub with numerous restaurants, cafés, tea-rooms and pubs as well as bookshops and antique and bric-a-brac shops (such as those of Robert Mucci, left, and Deeday White, above).

On the corner of the High Street and Courthouse Street is Reeves shop, one of the town's oldest businesses, which has been trading since 1818 (the socialist writer Robert Tressell, who based *The Ragged Trousered Philanthropist* on his life in Hastings, used to buy books here). Also in the High Street is the Flowermakers Museum.

Old Town

The Old Town Museum is located in the High Street. Housed inside the former town hall, it covers the history of the old town from the first neolithic settlements through to more recent times. On the ground floor a wealth of exhibits includes model boats, early photographs, maps, domestic scenes, and souvenirs prized by Victorian holidaymakers. The panelled upper gallery covers pre-Victorian times, including the smuggling trade, Tudor relics, the Cinque Ports era, and early settlements.

Noteworthy buildings in the High Street include medieval hall houses (at 97 and 102-3), the original 15th century Market House (42a), and the old bank building (90). The son of novelist Charles Dickens was a frequent visitor to No.112, which is why it's called Dickens Cottage. At the end of the High Street, the Stables Theatre stands on the site of the former stables of Old Hastings House.

On the eastern side of the valley, All Saint's Street features a raised pavement and a rich collection of wonderfully preserved buildings from the 15th and 16th centuries including the Stag Inn, an ancient hostelry with smuggling associations. The Cinque Port Arms, another venerable pub, dates from the 17th century. At the top of the street, All Saint's Church stands on a sloping site at what would have once been the entrance to Hastings (Titus Oates, who achieved notoriety during the fictitious 'Popish plot' in 1678, was a curate here).

Seagulls

The raucous squawk of seagulls is the definitive soundtrack to the seaside experience. Hastings' seagulls often amuse visitors with their cheeky attempts to pilfer from picnics on the beach but equally as often they irritate residents with their persistent mess and noise. It's best to give in gracefully - not only are they numerous but also, as wild birds, they're protected by law.

The most common species which nests on the town's rooftops is the herring gull. These large birds can attain a wingspan of nearly a metre and live for up to 20 years. The only other gull which sometimes nests on rooftops is the black-backed gull, which is similar in size and shape to the herring gull but darker in colour.

Breeding pairs court in April and start building their nests in May. Eggs are laid from early May onwards, with the first chicks appearing around the beginning of June. The chicks generally fledge in August. It's during these summer months, as the chicks and adults constantly call to each other from dawn onwards, that the gulls are at their noisiest.

Old Town Week

One of the most popular events in Hastings' calendar is Old Town Carnival Week, which has been going strong since 1968. This extravaganza of events is organised wholly by volunteers to raise money for charity. It includes everything from art installations to ghost walks and tug-of-war contests to a three-legged treasure hunt, culminating in the carnival itself. Displaying all the creative quirkiness and bohemian bonhomie for which Hastings is renowned, Carnival Week has a huge local, national and even international following.

For both participants and spectators, the entertainments available range from the sublime to the ridiculous. The 'pram race' for instance, features costumed teams who have to push their vehicles through the old town's streets, visiting 18 pubs along the way and stopping off in each one to discover the answer to a pre-set question. Not surprisingly, finding the answers can become increasingly difficult as the evening wears on.

The week starts with a grand opening procession and the hugely popular free beach concert, which showcases top local bands and raises money for the lifeboats. During the week there are also tours and open studios, gardens and houses, coffee mornings, lunches, recitals and art installations throughout the old town, as well as a street party and a blessing of the animals service.

On Friday evening the carnival fills the streets with sound, light and colour as dozens of groups parade their floats.

Old Town Week

Another local Old Town Week tradition is a bike race up Crown Lane, the old town's steepest road, to win the Jimmy Read Memorial Trophy (it commemorates a fisherman's helper, or 'boy ashore', who lost his life in the 1987 hurricane). From a standing start, entrants must pedal an old butcher's bike up the hill - without raising their bum from the saddle - on a timed run.

Hastings is home to a wealth of artists working in varied medias and techniques. Each year a local artist is invited to produce a work to illustrate a poster (this page and overleaf) promoting the bike race. Featured artists have included Martin Honeysett, Gus Cummins, Mick Rooney, Angie Braven, Laetitia Yhap, Pete Smith, Roland Jarvis and Linda King.

Old Town Week

Jimmy Read Memorial Trophy

Crown Lane 5.30 August 9th
Hastings Old Town 1994

Jimmy Read Memorial Trophy

HASTINGS '95

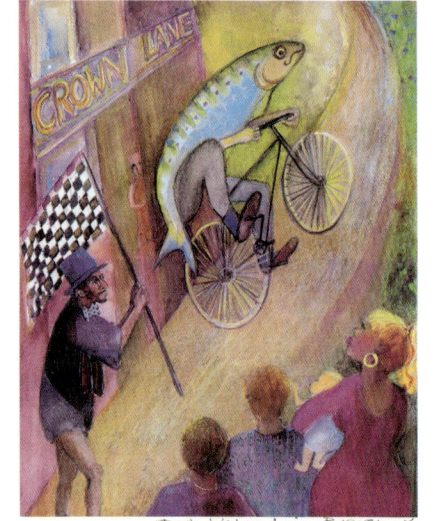

Jimmy Read Memorial Trophy

Hastings 1996

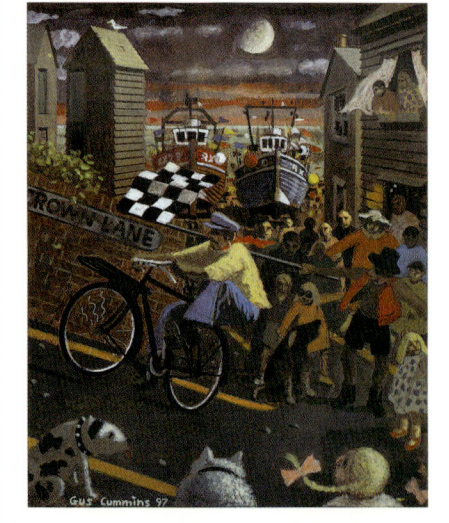

10th JIMMY READ MEMORIAL TROPHY

HASTINGS 1997

84

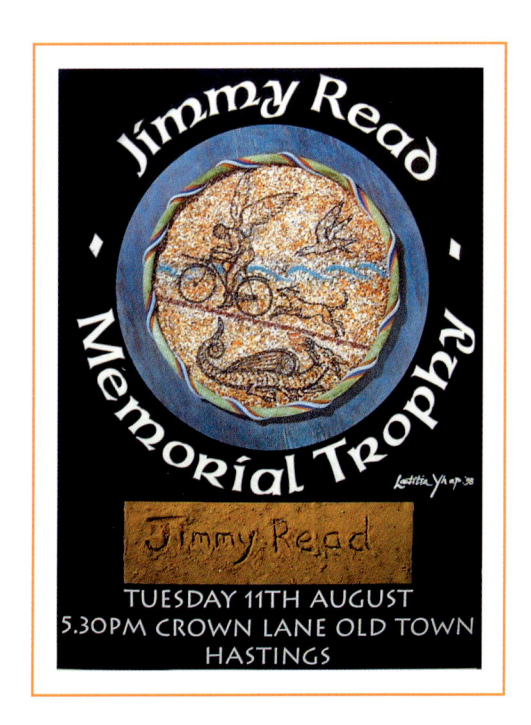

Jimmy Read Memorial Trophy

TUESDAY 11TH AUGUST
5.30PM CROWN LANE OLD TOWN
HASTINGS

12th Jimmy Reed Memorial Trophy - 1999
Tuesday 10th August 5.30 start
Crown Lane - Old Town - Hastings

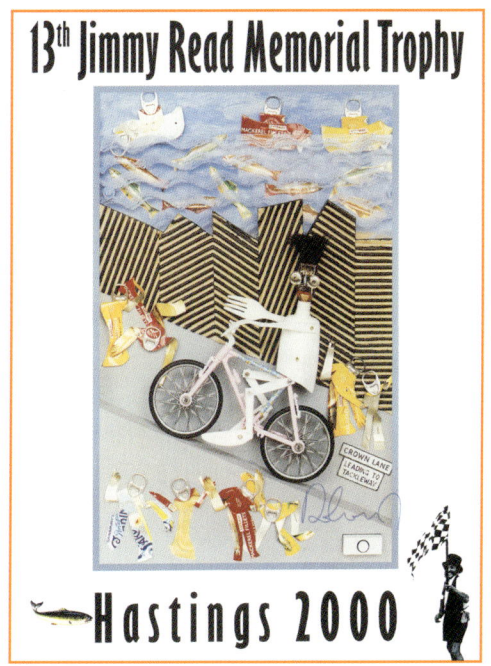

13th Jimmy Read Memorial Trophy
Hastings 2000

14th Jimmy Read Memorial Trophy
CROWN LANE TUESDAY 7TH AUGUST 2001 5.30pm

Old Town Week

On Sunday the fishing fleet is decked out in bunting for the hard-fought Fishing Boat Race, in which buckets of water and flour bombs are deployed ruthlessly between mirthful passengers as rival boats race from the Harbour Arm to the pier and back. It's a fun, lively finale to one of the community's best loved seasonal events.

The Stade

The Stade, Hastings' fishing quarter, has been in active use for centuries. Home to one of the country's oldest fishing fleets, still using traditional-style boats, the Stade has a maritime heritage which is unique in Britain.

The fishing quarter's name is derived from the Saxon word for landing place and primarily refers to the shingle beach where the boats are launched but also, by extension, to the whole area alongside Rock-a-Nore road beneath the East Hill.

At the core of the Stade is the fleet itself, which is the largest beach-launched fishing fleet in Europe. Several attempts have been made to build a harbour in Hastings, all of which have failed (the Harbour Arm, jutting out between the main beach and the Stade, is the remains of one such attempt). Consequently, the fishing boats continue to be launched from the beach. Tractors are used to launch and land them, and some are also hauled out by diesel-powered winches.

Because of the way the boats work, they cannot be much longer than 10 metres and therefore they can only carry relatively small amounts of fishing gear and travel short distances. As a result, the fleet has always fished in an ecologically sustainable way.

The Stade

The tall wooden sheds which line the shingle beach along Rock-a-Nore road are unique to Hastings. Known as net shops, these black sheds, mostly three stories high, were used for storing fishing nets and tackle. The beach where the net shops stand was much narrower in the last century than it is now. Consequently, the council allocated the fishermen just 2.5 square metres each to build their storage huts. Since there was a lot of gear to store, they had to build the sheds upwards. The reason that there are big gaps between them was to make space for the horse-drawn capstans which used to pull the boats back up the beach.

In years past the fishing community used to build elaborate archways using barrels, fish nets, oars and other materials to mark special occasions. This practice was revived to build a millennium arch (detail, far left), which was such a success that there are plans to create a more permanent reminder of this unique custom.

The Fishermen's Museum is housed inside a former church, built on the beach in 1854, which ministered to the fishing community. It provides a fascinating introduction to the town's fishing industry, with many marine curiosities and mementoes on display. The museum opened in 1956 and is run by volunteers from the Old Hastings Preservation Society. The centrepiece is a full-scale boat, the *Enterprise*, which is one of the last surviving examples of a sailing lugger.

The Stade

The Fishermen's Museum recently benefited from a £300,000 revamp which included the building of a new extension to house displays on fishing today. Outside the museum there are several historic boats including the *Edward and Mary*, the first locally built boat to be fitted with an engine, and the *Grace Georgina*, which was the last traditional clinker boat to be built in Hastings.

The Shipwreck Heritage Centre is an award-winning museum which focuses on the numerous ships which have been wrecked off the Hastings coast, with hands-on and interactive displays. Some of the more prominent ships featured include the 70-gun English warship *Anne*, which beached near Hastings in 1690, and the *Amsterdam* (see page 13).

Underwater World features over 20 themed displays which bring the fishy world of tidal rock pools, sandy seabeds, and other marine environments vividly to life. The centrepiece is a 15 metre glass tunnel which takes visitors beneath a dramatic 'reef pool' teeming with sharks, rays, crabs, and starfish. Underwater World is renowned for its breeding and conservation programmes (particularly with endangered sea horses) and there is always something new to see in the sea life nursery, such as these baby jellyfish (right).

Officially the steepest funicular railway in Britain, the East Hill lift runs from Rock-a-Nore up to top of the East Hill, from where there are spectacular views of the coastline.

The Stade

Fresh, locally-caught fish is a major appeal of the Stade. The top catches are mostly flat fish such as plaice, Dover and lemon sole, turbot and brill. Other important catches are cod and whiting. Skate, huss and monkfish are also landed. Seasonal catches include mackerel (summer), sea bass, squid and conger eel (summer and autumn), herrings (autumn) and sprats (late winter).

Locally-smoked fish are very popular, and traditional delicacies such as jellied eels, cockles, whelks, rollmops, oysters and crabs are available from seafood bars.

Coastal Currents

Coastal Currents, one of Britain's foremost festivals of contemporary visual art, runs throughout September and October. It provides an opportunity to view new work and exhibitions, often in original or unusual locations, as well as participate in workshops, talks, walks, and performances. A key element of this innovative festival is that numerous artists open up their houses, gardens and studios to give the public a unique insight into the creative processes at work (Roland Jarvis' studio, pictured left).

Events and exhibitions (most of which are free) encompass the whole coastline between Bexhill and Folkestone, with Hastings the focal point for many of the highlights. Coastal Currents also embraces photography, mixed media and digital art as well as the recently established Shot by the Sea film festival, which is a showcase for the thriving independent film culture in the town.

Fishermen

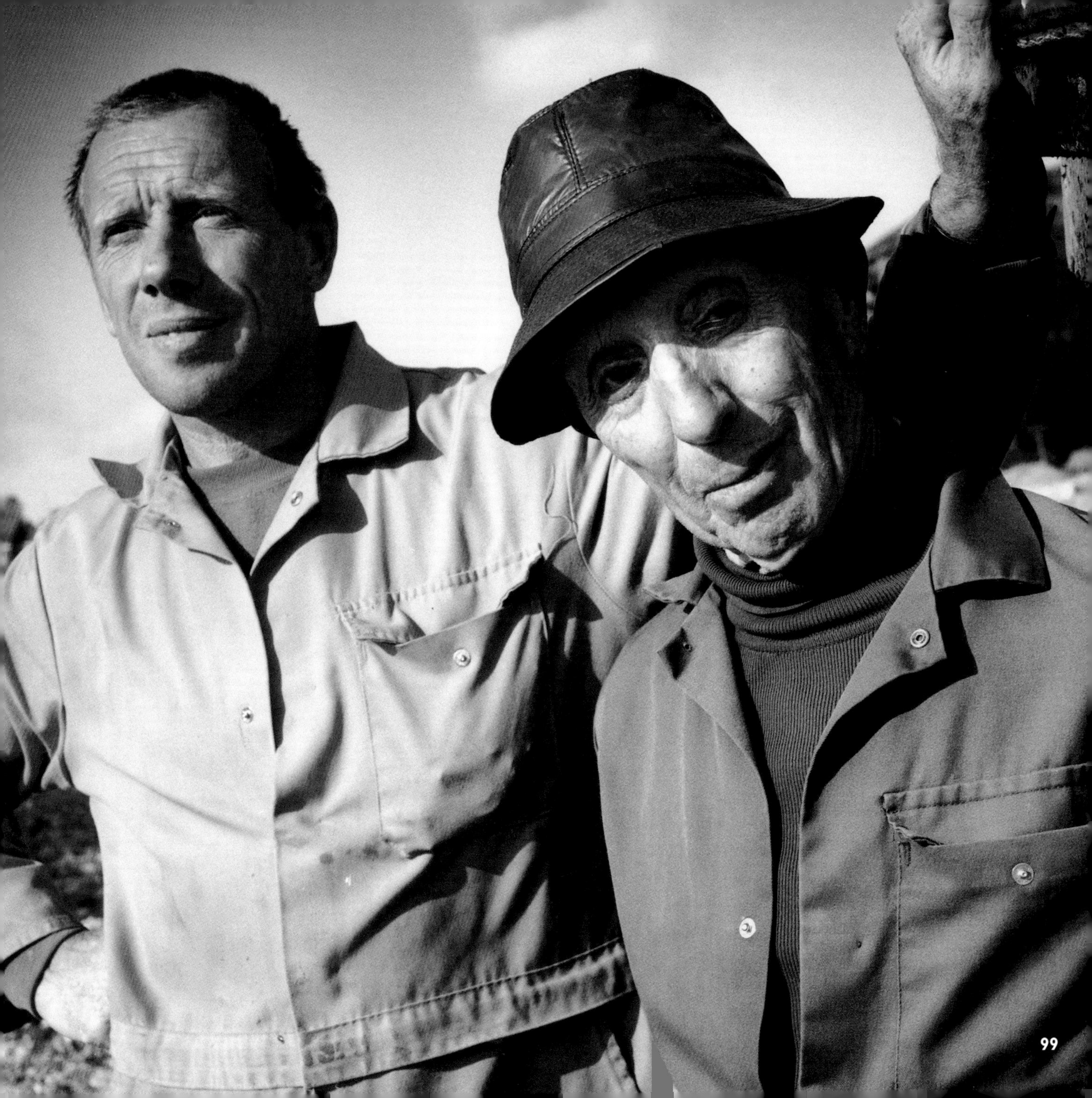

Fishermen

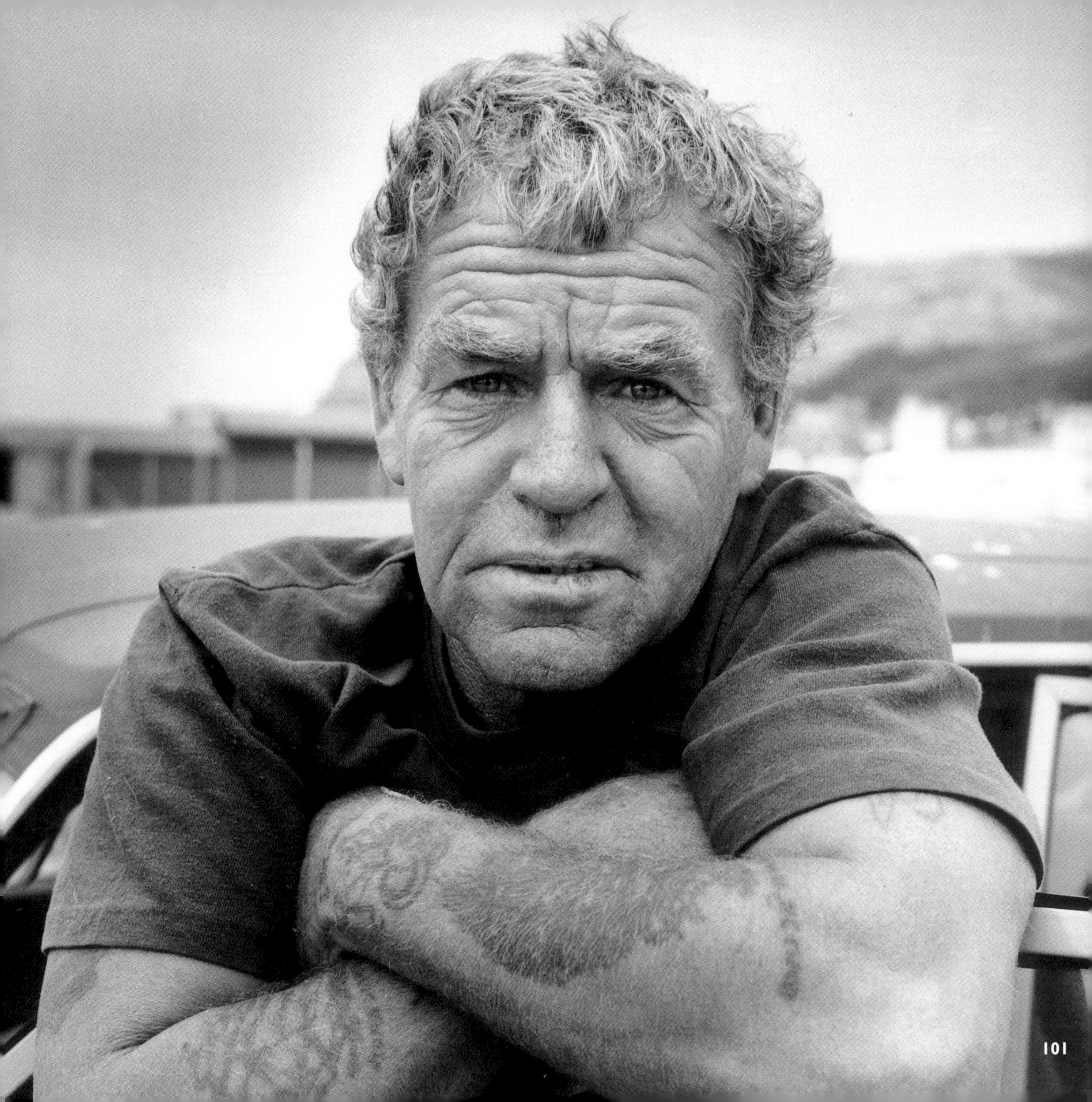

Fishermen

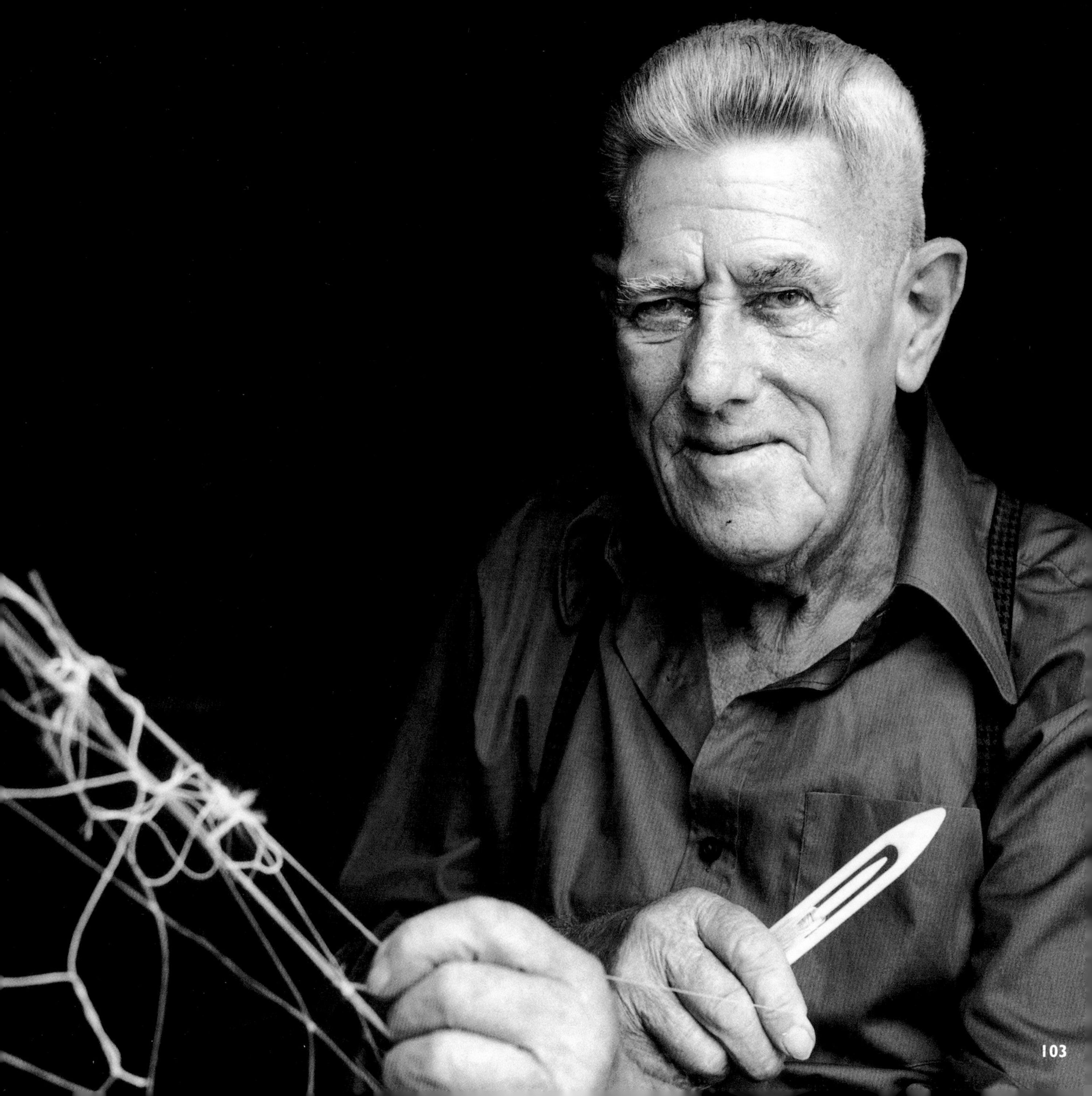

Hastings week

Hastings Week takes place during mid-October to mark the anniversary of the Battle of Hastings (October 14, 1066). The celebrations encompass a diverse range of entertainments and activities including jazz, classical, and brass concerts, poetry readings, art exhibitions, a town criers competition, and sporting events. The battle itself is re-enacted annually on Senlac Hill and William's victory is commemorated in the Gonfalon Ceremony, in which his pennant is ceremonially raised in the grounds of Hastings Castle. The week includes the Bonfire celebrations (see p108).

105

Urban Woodland

106

Hastings' largest urban woodland is St Helen's Park wood (right), which covers a surprisingly sizeable tract within the northern part of town. Most of it is ancient broadleaf forest comprising oak, beech, hornbeam, and alder, with abundant shrubs such as holly and hazel. There are also wildflower meadows in the middle of the valley. The 36 hectare (88 acre) park is maintained by the St Helen's Park Preservation Society.

Located in Hollington, Church Wood covers 17 hectares (42 acres) of similarly ancient broadleaf forest. Much of it is managed as coppice-with-standards woodlands; coppicing allows more sunlight into the wood, encouraging bluebells, wood anemones, butterflies, voles and lizards.

A chapel has existed here since at least 1090, and the foundations may be Saxon in origin. The nickname 'church-in-the-wood' has been in use since around 1777, although its proper name is St Leonard's Church.

On the west side of Queensway in Hollington is the less well-known Marline Valley Nature Reserve, which includes parts of Marline Wood, Park Wood, and meadowland. The Marline Valley is a steep-sided ghyll woodland cut through sandstone by the Marline stream: this humid environment supports a unique collection of rare ferns, mosses and liverworts. Yellow rattle, common spotted orchids and adder's tongue fern thrive in the wildflower meadows. This 40 hectare (99 acre) reserve, which is a Site of Special Scientific Interest (SSSI), is managed by the Sussex Wildlife Trust.

Bonfire

One of the major set-pieces of the year, the celebration of bonfire night is marked with the same creative gusto which the town brings to bear on other cultural events. Traditionally, it is scheduled during Hastings Week (see p104).

Throughout English history bonfires have been lit at times of commemoration. The original Sussex bonfires were lit in celebration of the deliverance of king and parliament from Guy Fawkes' Gunpowder Plot of 1605. Over the centuries Sussex Bonfire has become symbolic of the rights to free speech and the liberty of the individual, hence the practice of burning effigies of authoritarian figures (such as unpopular politicians, or even traffic wardens). In Hastings, a cross is also burnt on top of the bonfire as a memorial to everyone who has died defending the freedom of the individual.

Spectacular firework displays and a dramatic procession, complete with flaming torches and thumping drums, mark this hugely popular event, which is co-ordinated by volunteers from the Hastings Borough Bonfire Society and their percussionists, Monster's Drums.

Bonfire

HASTINGS BONFIRE

THIS ROAD CLOSED

SAT 14th OCTOBER
7.00pm – 10.00pm

**WARNING
LOUD BANGS
ON ROUTE**

Hastings Borough Bonfire Society

110

111

Bonfire

113

Country Park

The Country Park is one of Hastings' most treasured assets. Rising up behind the old town, it spans five kilometres of glorious cliff top views, moss-strewn ravines, heathland and woodland.

Covering 260 hectares (640 acres), the park lies within the High Weald Area of Outstanding Natural Beauty and is home to many interesting creatures including the grey bush-cricket, green hairstreak butterfly, green woodpecker, bank vole and wood mouse. Stonechats, whitethroats and yellowhammers nest in the prickly heathlands.

Seabirds are plentiful along the cliffs, with fulmars and cormorants nesting on their otherwise sheer faces. The cliffs themselves comprise some of the oldest rocks in the south-east of England, rich in plant and animal fossils. The park is also important archaeologically, with remains of Stone Age, Iron Age and Romano-British settlements.

The park starts at the East Hill, where a pitch-and-putt course extends below a picnic area which was once a large Iron Age fort. The first valley heading eastwards is Ecclesbourne Glen, a heavily-wooded ravine which is a fairyland of ferns, liverworts and mosses growing on the stream banks. It was once a major smuggling route.

The next valley is Fairlight Glen, an ancient woodland which is carpeted in spring time with an array of wildflowers including bluebells, wild garlic, red campion, yellow archangel and wood anemones.

Country Park

116

Fairlight Glen provides the only access within the park to the beach. Fairlight Beach is a popular naturist beach. Covehurst Wood, above the beach, was an ideal landing place for smugglers and the scene of several encounters between smugglers and coastguards at that time.

Beyond here is Warren Glen, home to numerous nesting songbirds and renowned for its fabulous displays of spring wildflowers. The final stretch of the park, known as the Firehills, is heathland (mainly comprising gorse, bell heather and bracken) with wonderful views across the Channel.

The Visitor Centre and main car parks are behind the Firehills, with other car parks on Fairlight Road and Barley Lane. The park can be reached on foot from the old town via the East Hill lift or by climbing the Tamarisk steps.

The park has two permanent rangers and a further 45 volunteers who help maintain the footpaths and bridges, monitor wildlife, and provide information for visitors. A wide-ranging events programme encompasses everything from countryside management to guided rambles, torchlight walks, badger watching, childrens' fun days, and mystery nights with local story-teller Ben Fairlight (left).

Christmas

Father Christmas arrives on his fishing boat, whilst Christmas decorations are lit up throughout Hastings and the pantomime season gets into full swing at the White Rock Theatre. The Fishermen's Museum is the venue for a traditional carol service (bottom right).

Photographers Credits

Photographs are listed alphabetically clockwise, as appropriate for each page.

Andrew Catlin: 30; 31; 63. **John Cole:** 6b,c; 7a; 14; 15b; 29a; 34d; 39a, b; 41b; 55; 56a,d; 57a,d; 67d; 68; 74; 75a; 80; 81b; 95a,b; 98; 99; 100; 101; 102; 103; 110c,e; 111a; 112; 113c; 118; 119a,b,c,d. **Tim Cross:** 19b; 25a; 26a; 34b,c; 43b; 52a; 56b; 71c; 72b; 73a; 79a,c; 97b,d; 110d; 115b; 117b. **Käthe Deutsch:** 91b. **Steven Differ:** 29b; 116. **George Greaves:** 13c; 28; 35a; 49a; 60; 78; 86; 88; 89a,c; 90b. **Peter Greenhalf and Janet Pollard:** 12; 13a; 24; 42; 58; 92b; 109. **Nick Hanna:** 6d; 7c,d; 10a; 13b; 15c; 17a; 18a; 19a,c; 21b; 23d; 25b; 26c; 27a; 32; 33b; 36; 37a,b; 38; 40; 41c; 43a,c,d,e; 49b; 50c,d; 52c; 53a,b,c; 61a; 64; 65b,c; 66; 67c; 70; 71b; 72a; 73b,c; 75b,c; 76b; 77a,b; 90c; 91a; 92d; 94a,b; 95c; 106a,b,c; 107a,b; 117c. **Roland Jarvis:** 92a; 96. **Peter Johns:** 69d; 87a. **John Kenward:** 69b; 79b. **Bob Mazzer:** 6a; 15a; 17b; 19d; 26b; 27b; 33a; 33c; 34a; 35b; 45b,c; 46a,b; 47; 52b; 56c; 57b; 59a,b; 65a; 67a,b; 81c; 87b; 97a,c; 104; 105a,b; 110a,b; 113b. **John Miles:** 7b; 79d; 81d. **Denise O'Neil:** 117a. **Chris Parker:** 16; 18b; 20; 21a; 22; 23a,b; 39c; 41a; 44; 45a; 48; 50a,b; 51; 54; 61b; 69a; 71a; 72c; 76a,d; 89a,b,c; 90a; 93; 108; 114; 115a; 116; 117a. **Steve Pyke:** 62a,b,c,d; 76c; 81a; 82; 83a,b; 92c. **Camilla Stapleton-Hibbert:** 111b; 113a. **Sussex Wildlife Trust:** 10b; 11a,b. **Nick Wates:** 23c. **Anna White:** 57c; 69c.

Front Cover: **John Cole:** b. **Nick Hanna:** d. **Peter Greenhalf and Janet Pollard:** c. **Chris Parker:** a.
Back Cover: **John Cole:** c. **Steven Differ:** d **Chris Parker:** a,b.

Bike race posters reproduced by kind permission of the Old Town Carnival Association.

For accomodation, travel reservations and further information, contact:
Hastings Information Centre, Queen's Square, Priory Meadow, Hastings, East Sussex TN34 1TN
Tel: 01424 781111   Fax: 01424 781186   www.hastings.gov.uk   E-mail: hic_info@hastings.gov.uk